Catalogue of Surprises

Catalogue of Surprises

Poems

Dorothy Wall

BLUE LIGHT PRESS ❖ 1ST WORLD PUBLISHING

SAN FRANCISCO ❖ FAIRFIELD ❖ DELHI

Catalogue of Surprises

Copyright ©2023 by Dorothy Wall

All rights reserved. Printed in the United States of America. No part of this book may be used or reproduced in any manner whatsoever without written permission except in the case of brief quotations embodied in critical articles and reviews. For information contact:

1ST WORLD LIBRARY
PO Box 2211
Fairfield, IA 52556
www.1stworldpublishing.com

BLUE LIGHT PRESS
www.bluelightpress.com
bluelightpress@aol.com

BOOK & COVER DESIGN
Melanie Gendron
melaniegendron999@gmail.com

COVER ART
Mel Davis, *River*

AUTHOR PHOTO
William Barnes

FIRST EDITION

Library of Congress Cataloging-in-Publication Data

ISBN: 978-1-4218-3551-8

Also by Dorothy Wall

Identity Theory: New and Selected Poems

Encounters with the Invisible: Unseen Illness, Controversy, and Chronic Fatigue Syndrome

Finding Your Writer's Voice: A Guide to Creative Fiction (coauthor)

Hanging the Mapmaker (chapbook)

Catalogue of Surprises

Nothing can ever happen twice.
In consequence, the sorry fact is
that we arrive here improvised
and leave without the chance to practice.

– Wislawa Szymborska

Table of Contents

1

Hemingway Puts Down His Gun . 1
Arriving . 2
Refrigerator on the Freeway . 3
My Grandson Wants to Go to Chernobyl . 4
Mr. Yu Reads the Headlines Before Dying . 5
Not Today . 7
Comes a Wasp . 8
Where to Find Hope . 10
Writing as Divination . 12
Haiku . 13

2

Spread . 17
Shelter . 18
Catalogue of Surprises . 20
News . 23
Travel Guide for the Slow . 24
This Morning . 26
Baby Born in Bomb Shelter . 27
New Year's Day . 28
After Church . 29
Between . 30
Notes on Destruction: Florentine Pieta . 32

3

All the Ghosts . 37
How to Survive . 38
Family History . 41
Truth . 42

Leaving . 44
The Maskless Face . 45
Not Only Diderot . 46
You Can't Trust Anybody These Days, Can You? . 47
I'm Right . 48
It's True . 50
Slippage . 51
It Isn't Enough . 52
The House We Built . 53
Pickings . 54

4

Three Boats and a Silence . 57
Morning Walk . 59
Towhee on the Flagstone . 61
Intelligence . 62
Trinity Mountains . 63
Circling . 65
Dispatch from the Eighth Decade . 66
These Days . 67
Hospital Dreams . 68
Laws of Motion . 70
To Carve . 72
To Whom It May Concern . 73
Afterlife . 74
Notice . 76
22nd Century Poems . 78
The Fight We Have Left . 79

Acknowledgments . 81
About the Author . 83

To Bill, for accompanying me

1

Hemingway Puts Down His Gun

I read the story somewhere, how each day
he tried to stop writing when he knew

what came next

As long as words, strong as a rope
hauled him into another day

he knew he'd keep going
If you ever thought words can't save us

think again: a string of words
a suspension bridge

a rope we've tied ourselves to
above the chasm

You'd think I'd understand this rope-pulled
undertaking, this aerial act, but I don't

this trusting at the edge that requires
trusting yourself, now that's

scary. Below the river flits from green
to blue, darker at the bend

where words end
until

Arriving

> "Water ticked and added up to time."
> – *Why Time Flies*, Alan Burdick

I'll settle for obsolescence, Lone Ranger
and Tonto still the password my husband uses,
part of the shrinking posse who know

the magic of those words. I resist endings,
who doesn't, though the miserly universe drips
its daily count. Look at my neighbor

promenading, baby melded to her chest. Look
at those tiny bare limbs, loose as hung sausage
asleep to effort, not questioning their purchase

on the world. It's the distance left that's maddening
mine shortening each time she struts the street
her belly pack sweeping ahead like a procession

announcing a queen which at this moment she is.
Her impending demise I keep to myself this peaceful
afternoon in her kingdom. I have no need to tell her

of the water clock's slow drip, that vessel
draining with each hour, each step.
The water line falls, no one sees where it goes

only that it's gone like milk summoned
by a baby's tongue, drop by drop when she wakes
ravenous to the world.

Refrigerator on the Freeway
Traffic report, "Morning Edition," NPR

All the scattered calamities we leave
behind, those migrations leaving their trail

of chaos, saltwater intrusion in Louisiana
marshes, ice-free winters in the Bering Sea

another spring of beeless
trees, the heave of a king tide over

washed-out walks, but who can slake
that thirst raking through each of us.

Someone is waiting for their refrigerator.
Wandering and unplugged, we're left

to find a new route home
like that Atlantic gannet off the coast

of San Francisco who may
or may not remake its world. To you

still searching for your appliance
it will arrive soon

humming, latched, so you
can believe in repair.

My Grandson Wants to Go to Chernobyl

He wants to see what feeds on disaster,
foxes, roe deer, wild boar, bison,

polecats and mink, thriving without us.
Thirty-seven years since everyone

scattered, as if by advancing troops that seek
only us. We want to be exceptional, so we are.

Why are we surprised at reversal, ravens
nodding from windows, no one to harvest lettuce

but the fat hares. A fertile derangement, woodlands
spreading, fresh heaps of teeth-carved birch

as beavers rework their streams, a new world
let loose the day everyone fled.

Sure, they've found albino barn swallows and voles
with cataracts, but life still outwits the dead,

persistence its own form of beauty.
Why wouldn't he want to enter that garden?

Mr. Yu Reads the Headlines Before Dying
    Obituary in the *San Francisco Chronicle*, name changed

It didn't look good, anyone could see,
the wounded world he was leaving
like smoke leaves fire, polluted,

scorched, its lung-wound slow and inside.
Someone who cares for him has left
the window open. He sees

in direct sight, daffodils, blaringly
yellow, their perfect megaphone
faces so sure of themselves,

little thickets springing forth,
reliable as the insufferable parade
of cheerfulness that attends the ill.

Those always ready faces
still offering their full cups
as if ruined earth were hospitable

that old body that gives and gives
despite what we've done, despite
what's coming, as if no one sees

it giving up, giving out, and we could
all shoot up from tidy bulbs
and begin again.

When I read the obit, like a banner in the sky,
I want to shout, Mr. Yu! Mr. Yu!
We're down here learning resuscitation,

hands in the soil, trying to revive that
struggling body, trying to be honest like you,
though honestly, we prefer to be fooled.

Not Today

While damage unmoors and upends,
we go to the pool. I don't swim,
I watch, a glaring water-light my granddaughter
dives under, hair streaming and sleek.
It's easy here. Water chlorine-clean,
untouched by brown torrents gushing,
waterfall heavy, through Kentucky streets,
tearing into basements, taking down houses,
power lines, SUVs, like the house of cards they are.
The truth, the wet truth. In Pakistan a deluge
devours hillsides, houses, lives. Maldives' beaches
disappear, gigantic bites. Here a shimmer
of blue popsicle puddles on cement.
Child voices in splashy play.
                    A reckoning hovers
above the gleaming water like an Old Testament
prophet scolding and hurricane huge, ready to
bind us in his furious arms.
Eventually. Not today.

Comes a Wasp

Another wanderer through our lives,
in and out our bedroom window

and should we stop her (meaning me,
husband being distracted)?

Had she been more tidy she
might have prevailed but

splatted mud shagged the walls,
careless trail, and on

the sconce that mud-mound
stuck fast, growing bulge laid

daub by muddy daub, building up
as afternoons one after another

wear down. Here I pause.
Husband wanders in, gone

again. It's the next
generation I wonder about,

and that hapless spider
paralyzed and interred inside

for the pupa to eat alive.
Who am I to lament or decide? I break

the hardened knob off its
metal plate, a halved womb clutching

a ridged, pearly cocoon
doubly cradled and not enough

to save it. She returns for days, nosing
other dubious corners, caroms off

tending and abandoning, she's not
lost like us, no quivering on the brink

or over-think, just zoom, zoom
her long, weaving drive

to seed some other mud-pocked
unfurling life.

Where to Find Hope

> "The phrenologists already knew that hope was situated
> in the prefrontal cortex: 'in front of conscientiousness,
> and behind marvelousness, being elongated in the direction
> of the ears.'"
> – "Electrified," by Elif Batuman, *The New Yorker*, April 6, 2015

Clearly I've been searching all the wrong places
trekking through uncertainty, lost
in absurdity.

My fingertips wander to the precise spot, massaging scalp
like a clairvoyant her crystal or a mother her baby's
fontanelle, still open

Skeptical self, please believe in the possible

      against evidence
Everyone's tired of the news, fill my head
with something else

a map clear as a phrenologist's staked claim
      giving us not only discovery
            but faith. I don't need

answers, just beginnings, like that infant
      newly swum up from its bath
           of stem cells that can be anything
      heal anything

that swarm to where they belong
doing what they're meant to
           unbewildered

their orchestrated flood, like hope
       changing
              what they touch
in the beginning.
What we do next is what matters.

Writing as Divination

From the fortunes ancient Chinese read in inscriptions
on turtle shells or oracle bones, those
broken lines, angular carvings.

Writing was born from longing, touching a future
in an animal's left-behind home.

Longing to know the fruits and terrors stretched
in long rows before us like an orchard or graveyard set
in the same indecipherable soil.

Longing for a glimpse through the cracked door
where that not-yet self flickers,
        a finger trace away.

And when those seekers wrangled open that door
did they find what they wanted?
No, they abandoned that ransacked home
        (who ever wants what they find)
made their own

out of those broken lines
and carvings, forked river beds
and curves

came written words
this multiplicity.

Brushstrokes that shape
anything imaginable.

Worlds of our own making.

Haiku

It's when you have 5 syllables, 7 syllables, 5,
and it's about nature or a season, and disjuncture
because that's how life is, whatever you see
there's always a juxtaposition, like

a skinny-haunched dog
pissing in slick snow, a hiss
of steamy beauty
               that's one,
and so this scraggly, flea-bitten
urine-smelling world has these moments when

you laugh and that steamy piss-drilled snow hole
is beautiful, it's what life is. Crazy.

It has green peaches and cuckoos and moonlight
and things like that, so you might say

evening light on the
        old cuckolded cuckoo, its
rain-drenched cries fade

now that's a sad one, not so funny, but
it's another world we can
carry around and wonder about and that's

the thing, kids get this really fast, since they
wonder about everything, they want to taste
that green peach, and why is it bitter
and can you use cats, and were there cats in Japan

and suddenly you're all opening that folded envelope sent
in spite of despair, biting into a ripe pear.

2

Spread

> "Governor Gavin Newsom issued a stay at home order...to slow the spread of COVID-19." – March 19, 2020, Sacramento

Then it wasn't safe
to laugh on porches,

I couldn't extend
my hand in greeting

future vague as a sideways
thought, as the distant haul-trucks

on I-5, their bulk a strange
reminder of hidden cargo.

As long as rain washes the low
hills wrapped in their

green pelt this late March,
we delude ourselves that

swiftness isn't the way
of life, contagion

won't overtake the ordinary
hours. Life through a window pane

dread of insidious guests
silent as a powder puff

chalking my face
that residue we laughed off

in ordinary times. Alarm comes
nightly now with its low rumble.

Shelter

    PBS "NewsHour," April 19, 2020

Animal shelters emptying as our houses
fill. A young girl and mother in NYC

grabbed a calico named Hillie
nosing a brood, five of them,

one hot in the girl's palm which helps
the way heat on a bruise helps.

When there's so much to heal we rely
on the smallest of hearts, knocking its

rapid pulse in a cupped hand as if panicked
though deep in a non-pandemic sleep.

The girl's face rapturous, quiet.
Shelter keeps surprising me with its two faces –

the one stifles, the other saves – and its many
guises, like a garden stumbled into around a bend.

Out in the city, sirens. A world we reel from
each night and can't recognize come morning,

fodder for a virus leaping into the human sea
as we dive into the ocean because it's there

and we can, without thought or purpose
but to live another day. Shelter

the opposite of wander, a place to pause
protected, as by a shield. In an apartment

in NYC a mother and daughter.
Hardwood floors. Kitties

slip-sprawling to mama's teats,
eyes closed for the moment.

Catalogue of Surprises

What happens in a house
doesn't stay in a house.
A virus enters and leaves
as the wanderer it is, following
the lure of new realms,
expanding its territory
while mine shrinks to these
rooms. It's the wanderings
within I didn't expect,
cellular shifting, these guests
that stay, altering the body
like a birthmark or your
children. What happened?
A virus flew in my mouth,
burrowing, roaming,
remaking my world. That's
what they do
superbly.

Catalogue of Plans

Your perfectly pressed jacket
a party you showed up for the
wrong day. I once talked
to a mother about being a parent
everything accidental she said
everything. No plan. Who could
plan what we end up with?
Haphazard as a virus that takes
any portal as invitation to settle
like spores exquisitely suited
to root, survive. What happens

in a body stays in a body.
My doctor thought that couldn't
happen. A virus seen only
by the damage it does,
object of endless argument.
Is it alive? Is it still alive?
It wakes, stirs, ravages
what else matters?

Catalogue of Accidents

These days my mind's a
nighttime desert, uninhabited
space, black and grey,
slowing perhaps, some
robber baron's stealthy work.
Blitzed with serotonin,
my dreams glittered alive,
poofed-up hair sprayed
magenta, neon blue, brash,
loud, laughing at me for
what the brain can do apart
from consent. All that
iridescent hair, coated over,
I was underneath. If
serotonin can change me why
not a virus? I don't know
the doctor said, not
to that question.

Catalogue of Acquisitions

Viral reservoir makes me think
of held water. The ability to fill
all crevices, to take the shape
of the host, eroding what was.

Embedded, a cunning permanence.
Can robber barons be controlled
and regulated or do you have
to get rid of them? There are
different versions of progress.
How to adapt. I'm becoming
more hospitable, letting
what barges in find its
way. Nighttime wandering
doesn't seem to matter.
Glitter gone, storms settling.
What happened? I haven't
figured out wholeness or
these visitors that stay.
Perhaps that viral virility
puffers down with time
dulled and senescent
its mark fading. Perhaps
we'll grow used to
each other, until our needs
coincide and I can't discern
the stranger inside.

News

How long have you lived
a fiction of bodies that don't

weather and split from
years of rain, denied

that entropy defines us, dissolution
not a question in your mind,

not a glimmer. Rusty and drifting,
metallic flakes trail you

daily, sad evidence you can't
sweep aside. Recognition

smothers like a thick blanket
pinned tight, no crack or slit

to see outside this woolly
dark that comes to sit

within, overtaking
simple suppers, grocery lists.

You forgot toothpaste, milk,
thought you'd drive

to the store tomorrow.
What faith.

Travel Guide for the Slow

Savanna, moraine, cloud forest –
why trample distant places?

Stay close to a trail of your own
making, a local footpath

that assures return, a staying
place. I move through the trail

the trail moves through me,
I find ahead and behind

where I'm going, where
I belong. Why look further?

A trail subsides, takes a breath
turns to follow itself again

content with its familiar
dust-lacquered pebbles

stepped and stomped
each time more settled in its

trailness, the world as full
and far as the slick

silvery snail-trail
that wanders and wavers,

a shimmer-sign appearing
in each morning's light,

that sidewalk glisten-trail
of last night's

travels. Why want more?
It's damp this morning

dirt-damp in the air.
I set out.

This Morning

It's as if the moment of sunfall on bedroom shades won't end

It's as if "Hakuna Matata" won't stop blasting between drops as my granddaughter showers

It's as if I can hold each note, wet and curvaceous in my palm

It's as if we're not on the brink and we can, all of us, be sloppy with our songs, toss them with no consequence but joy. She's not gulping coal dust but some child is. It's as if we can stand and listen instead of stopping to sweep the dust around our feet or demanding everyone come sweep with us or storming the headquarters where ruin is planned under a different name.

It's as if we have time. This morning *The Lion King*, yesterday *Hamilton*, 230-year-old drama alive in her throat, washed by water, she belted out "Burn!"

Baby Born in Bomb Shelter
PBS "NewsHour"
Kyiv, Ukraine, February 26, 2022

Gaping holes where life had been,
that life now underground and shaken.
Shuddering walls, light bulbs, a child pulled
tighter. The girl asleep on cement shifts and curls
back to her other world

one she conjures no matter
what disappears
or appears here in the birthroom
when one cry stops
the other begins
its stay

regardless of damage
settling now on mother's chest like water
on a wound, cleansing,
delivered. A woman pats the thin
blanket, TV camera angles
to the pinched face

inside, eyelids squeezed, unseeing,
she who we love instantly for her lack
of everything, knowledge
most of all. More explosions.

We turn our eyes to this tiny
wailing mouth, its indignation and will.
No one says anything. Everyone listens.

New Year's Day

If the most generous act is to ask nothing of another
which is to say to ask for nothing, I have failed

and again
        I ask why we can't blast this globe of light
into a different orbit like slamming a rocket into
an asteroid to shift its deadly trajectory, avoid collision.
We got Larry's email he thinks it's time to eat his
corned beef sandwich what he wants to do before he dies.
Evenings and minutes swerve into another place, another
meaning. I watch their disappearance like drying dampness
unrecoverable why am I thinking this way, mulling evaporation
a dry summer while speeding through space. I'm writing this
to prove it is possible to make something exist, to make that
tiny adjustment that assures survival on this the quietest day
of the year, full now of roar and rumble. Death tricks us
into thinking of vastness, stars and years, thousands
of calendar pages fluttering like confetti on a parade but really
it's small as a life funneled down to last things, small as a
sandwich, from Saul's perhaps, known for succulent
corned beef, a briny aftertaste on the tongue you linger over.

Early morning light, gingkos fluttering their bright display.
On this day regaled for the stretch of blankness ahead,
each day an empty room to be filled
                I grab my coat, ask for reason to hope
                      ask, ask.

After Church

Like any lost place, I still see it,
light-streaming windows, scarlet, pale blue

burnished walnut pews, polished shoes
      I can't link with anything
resembling a saved world.

How can you miss something you don't want to
return to, a music you keep tossing overboard
that comes gusting back like a scratchy wind.

In the house of faith and so much I didn't learn.

My mother once said she didn't feel anything
when praying. A confirmation. Sprawled

on my childhood bed, L.A.'s held-in heat
anointed my sweaty face.

Heavy metallic-screened air. Lips moving
to charge prayer with some flicker of life.

I peered into the hot night through a slit of pulled-back drape.

Streetlights, shadowed jacaranda, hoarse laughs shuttling
the neighbors' poker game through flung-open windows,
      such a near and foreign world.

My pale room floated, unseen, a tide carrying me out,
baptized and unprepared.

Between

Before departure, the last
boarding, why not visit
a long cool night, a nameless street
my father's razored haircut
his thin enigmatic scar.
I stared and stared at the base
of his skull where the scalpel
left its clean swift bite.
From the backseat as he drove
our '57 Chevy, I wondered at its
delicacy, a thin white line down
his bare neck I now know
is the line between life and
death that deft hands navigate
as we steer our way
dipping hands into bodies
briefly.

::

Some evenings I wonder how much is left.
Some evenings I watch the sky, each grey
horizon, fog bank, darkness
advancing as the mind does
or the surgeon's hands finding
exactly where the tumor lay
one deed allowing another as if
there's a purpose though I don't believe
there is. We wonder at imperfection
then at what is saved, which includes
in this case me, that car ride
that scar that says someone

touched the living flesh
inside, sutured tight two flaps
to close the mystery
and leave.

Notes on Destruction: Florentine Pieta

    Begun when Michelangelo was 72, intended as his tomb-piece, worked on for 8 years before he smashed it in a fit of frustration

What I saw first was weariness,
Nicodemus's half-lidded eyes
cast down at what we've done

blood and thorns.

An arm around each, N. labors to hold up the two Marys
who hold Him, fallen between them, His leaving
forestalled by their embrace and by symmetry
        because order still exists
                in this moment before.

N. was the one who spoke to me,
his eyes beneath his hood glazed by inner vision,
        and Mary with her unending job,
           shouldering faith.

I was tired, too, a secular fatigue, having long ago left belief
on the workshop floor. I didn't count on how hard it is
to hold out against collapse, though
                that's what we do in the end, or try.

::

Nicodemus's crew, their eyes
from another place
        where pain has already happened
only enduring left

M.'s first mallet smash was to the center, the heart.

::

Surrender doesn't release fatigue
but lets it be felt, cold to the touch as
veined marble M. couldn't save
His lap-flung leg wrongly placed
      resurrection too much effort
like the weary effort of supporting the dead

for us as for M.
never finished.

N.'s worn face never gracing M.'s tomb
eternally mirroring
us instead

M's moment of walking away, raging at stone
unmatched to vision, and isn't that
when we should not abandon each other?

::

Despite every error, that hooded figure braces
against dissolution to hold them all,
me, us, all in our incompleteness

Our children and theirs will find Him
in His mother's lap, the dead
refusing burial, His body lingering

so we can face imperfection
as if all the failures we collect
and discard, ignoring their trail
behind us, endure

held up for anyone, past and future
who knows the need to make from loss
something solid.

In the Museo dell'Opera del Duomo creation
is noisy as a hammer blow.

::

Strange to not believe but love the story,
or M.'s story,
or the story left behind,
their woven-armed, encircling grasp
      held so unrelentingly

Mary straining through stone
to cradle His head in a devotion that rivets and exhausts.

Endings are not
when things stop, hearts, hands, effort
      one blow, two

even endings continue.

3

All the Ghosts

At first they pestered until I implored them to leave.
Now they don't come and I call them back.
Where are they these long days past counting
since their voices broke the day into
its proper pieces? Where is the rightness
of them in their place, dishes clattering when you
expect them to, where they stood by the sink
each night, where I now stand, this rotation,
and how much longer?

How to Survive

> For my great-grandfather Frank Thomas Wall, 1861-1931, who twice lost his mind, the second time after the Great Mississippi Flood of 1927

FT's undoing the story goes,
the Great Mississippi Flood unleashing
monstrous swell and surge, flooding the gullet

of his Louisiana plantation, his eyes disbelieving
so much could be swallowed
fir and pine thrashing specks on a
roof-top river, an epic sea wrongly placed,
outbuildings, bungalows, strange shipwrecks.

Surveying the deluge, did he step
from his Ford, grasp the door handle
as if clinging to the drowned,
sinking already

into the hurricane inside him
torrents he loosed on grandma's
clapboard house on the Ouachita River,
every corner drenched in his muddy rain.
He can't stay, she said.

::

At Central Louisiana State Hospital for the insane,
when help was short, they wheelbarrowed
the dead to a garden plot, blank
gravestones in rows marking
the disgrace of bones sunk in this ground.

On March 10, 1928, the warden
timed his watch, stamped the papers.

FT would be housed, tended
as a grave is tended.

Even named, stone etched
to last 10,000 storms,
a grave is anonymous, quiet
in its decay as a mind
dissolved is noisy, never settled.
How could he not be restless?
Did he pace those mounded graves
where sunflowers wagged
their heads, or hover
in a doorway grabbing lungfuls
of damp Louisiana air –
I don't want to leave him there.

::

To bring back my great-grandfather
you'd have to pull him from water
but once a mind is submerged
it's changed in a way you can't recover
or forget. The year he starved himself it was

work that saved him, scrubbing
the pine floor until day by day
he emerged drying in the sun,
his body thinner, water wrung out,
no less mean but not so sodden.
He found his way to Grayling Creek,
yanked trout from deep currents into our

unforgiving world, bloody mouths
hung from his thumb,
the Montana sky large enough
to absorb all that's dark
and dripping, until the water

rose again. My grandfather
resurrected him twice, shaking him back
into time, though once you've died
and returned there's a precedent,
harder to outdo. The second time

didn't last, his mind too bloated
to float him through.
Everyone knew. Too late
for the miracle of evaporation
or even a clean dry shirt.
And I who never knew him
trying to haul him back
in this my own slim time.

Family History

That visit in 1984, when my cousins taped our grandfather showing photos of his Louisiana plantation, his off-hand words,

Yeah, and I went down there in 1920... and there I am on horseback riding around the plantation, and here's my little pickaninny friends, and there's nigger Jim, and there I am at the...

And M. said, *You wouldn't dare call them that today*, and granddad said, *No*, and did anyway, after which they set aside brutal history for dinner.

My other grandfather wouldn't let his daughter marry a Jew, my aunt complained about the Mexican receptionist, why don't they speak better English, and believe me, those aren't the only stories I uncover in our stash of family letters.

Well, they're all dead now, my cousin says, but not that dead, more like a curtain that drops after a finale, then the actors emerge grinning and bowing, still in costume, with their made-up faces stepping into today

like his recorded voice, still alive, just a little scratchy, my ear to the tape, listening closely, thinking perhaps I could leave a blank, why give the words second life, but I can't erase the truth of what I come from, what came before and what still pains, the casual comments that dismiss 400 years of brutality and inhumanity, I need to listen, acknowledge, condemn these words I transcribe, from his mouth to my typing fingers this day in 2022 when we no longer say that but it's never unsaid.

Truth

Story

Start with a photo, the kind Barthes says you can't
walk by without a ripple of disturbance.

My grandfather scowling, four somber children
in ruffled dresses, pressed trousers, an undaunted

small smile grandma pushes forward against
the turbulence of that family's gale.

A photographer's pyramidal perfection,
little Mary the apex, standing on a dais
              her deep frown flanked
by seated parents. Three others step
down left and right.

The Egyptian grandness of their sadness
              mythic, arranged
their unchanged lives before our eyes daily

like a kept vow you almost
begin to trust

Disturbance

Such stoicism awaits absurdity, arriving this morning,
after eighty-four years
              a silverfish
seeking a crack of darkness, finding its slithery way

through tortoise-shell frame
scrabbling behind glass over a whole family's

endurance, a wiggly dance by one who could
yet escape, whose wanderings into other lives
hint at subterfuge, infiltration
a chance undoing

Action

Here the story pauses. I was not in the room
to witness the odd tracings across faces
resembling my own. My grandson
discovered the unexpected.

A future conservationist, unaware
of what story he was writing over

or revealing, he inserted a knife-point
to guide the bug out of the maelstrom
        as if the story could be changed.

A messy business.

Ever After

That Christmas tableau of 1936 now adorned
by a butchered silverfish, those wispy antennae,
delicate filaments spraying outward

from an unruly smudge just above
my grandfather's glare, my father's neutral stare
I pass with a chill
all the years to follow.

Leaving

When I told myself I wasn't going back
it wasn't a lie exactly more like something
you have to say whether it's true
or not – how can you leave the ungone –
something the moment calls for
and you oblige the moment and the
upwelling inside, like a wave erasing
your footprints you have to find
someplace else to stand while you're
being washed away. And there you are.

                I still return
in that way we do without being there
exactly. And there you are.

No matter how long we keep trudging
straight-line ahead we always find
ourselves sinking into that undertow
burying toes, ankles, like old artifacts.
You think you're immune to history
but it always wins its slow victory.

The Maskless Face

"...the ocean shows us what we really are"
– "Our Lady of Recovery," Czeslaw Milosz

As do our faces
newly unveiled
not new as a baby,
more like an old brooch
prodding a memory
of the person who used
to wear it. Faces
you have to meet again
like staring into a mirror above
the bar, a swarm of faces
you don't recognize,
yours, strangely peering,
that moment your eyes
meet, startled, until you see
a second face peeling free
of before, dangerously.
The impulse to turn away,
cover or leave the taunt
of a bare face exposed,
that moving mouth.
Whose face? When you pivot
you face the world.

Not Only Diderot

> "A sensitive man, such as myself, overwhelmed by the argument leveled against him, becomes confused and doesn't come to himself again until at the bottom of the stairs," leaving the gathering.
> – Denis Diderot

I, too, have stumbled down those
stairs of chagrin, who hasn't,
that clever retort flashing after
the audience whirls away,
your forlorn flag waving in an
empty sky. *L'espirit d'escalier*
haunts the staircase as you leave
the party, follows you home,
settles in for a gloomy Bordeaux
bitter with regret, shortcomings
failures. Ah, to be quick
with answers perfected to
combat any challenge. Not only
stairs bring pangs, also beds
dinners, cities, the past
sequestered behind that shut door
leaking with old music
you're dying to hear again
so you can be ready.

You Can't Trust Anybody These Days, Can You?
    Last line in 1993 finale of soap opera "Eldorado"

You had to be ready, friends piled on the couch, cold Pepsi
and smoky BBQ, ready for the exploding sports car,
swaggering Tandy's miraculous return,

taking his place among those defying the forces of the universe
with a smirk. Seventy-two years of "Guiding Light" tallied
seven paralyzed, ten incestuous scandals, fifteen dead, all
reappearing, casually intact, to scandalize again, marry,
divorce, remarry

rebirth easy as a
lazy draw on a Marlboro.

We are so ready to believe.
Not easily dissuaded from conviction that life can continue,
nonchalant and clothed in buckskin fringe,
after the conflagration

the carnage only prelude to a smug delight
in transcendence
illusion embraced and trusted as Santa.

You who diddle over petty concerns, your mortgage
and dry skin,
            you who haven't leapt into that car, driven
off a Florida bridge, been washed up on a Caribbean shore,
married a prince only to be pitched into the ocean by his
evil brother and again dragged by currents to the U.S.

you who doubt the indomitable capacity in each
throbbing heart

can't imagine the thrill of reruns.

I'm Right

> "I have been wrong the wrong sex the wrong age
> the wrong skin the wrong nose the wrong hair the
> wrong need...."
> – "Poem About My Rights," June Jordan

Right size right skin right nose right thin
      right kin doors open to let me in.
Right clothes degrees DNA
      amazing the lift when you're seen this way.

Why should I
Why should you not
A question whose hot
      embers singe

my well-built house that's built
on your not

I sleep and wake
      in a teetering room

raking and dragging
      through that old
            scorching tune

that thin, that skin

the world's searing centrifugal spin
separating layers
whiteness pushed to the top

where it cannot
in fairness

      stay
and who decides
and who gets to say

and what in the hell is everybody being reasonable about[1]

---

1. "Poem About My Rights," June Jordan

It's True

the shears were in the shed
but if for you they were not

if they had never
existed except in the minds

of others – you're sure you would
know if they were ours –

and if they couldn't have cut
the brambles from this

thicket it's just as well
they're not here since the

cutting they've done has
become a thing apart

like the shears in the shed
you've never seen before.

Slippage

A hand loosening its grip
        is still a hand.

Two eggs for breakfast. A plastic smell.

We're not like that, we have
        interesting thoughts
                a certain detour is all

and did I already salt
                my egg

on what basis

        this morning a wandering through
            language, words

        sliding free as pennies on
                stairs, bright
promising, but strange

down there.

It Isn't Enough

to have a good heart,
even the good have bitter

pockets, even those,
as if weighted by stones,
      can't be unloaded
so easily.

I'm free, my mother sobbed
on the phone when
      her husband left
I can come help you

but I knew her flung heart
wasn't meant to serve me,

her hand extended
for me to lift her from
      grief, from what failed.

It's late, I told her.
Get some sleep.
      Too late to tackle
the sadness of our imperfections,

those pitted places that won't
dislodge, that announce
who we are
      trying not to be.

The House We Built

> The house is "the topography of our intimate being"
> – Gaston Bachelard

In that first room, every floorboard lavished
every corner gleaming with the tenderness

before light. In the second an open window
to toss out old blames, rattling boxes

we didn't need and wouldn't remember.
I didn't linger enough in that air.

That third room where rivers run, torrents
of grievance tearing through spaces

we thought salvaged, an upending
we couldn't have seen before

the fourth room, its defiance bled away
by the coveted sharp object we hid in

the last room where a gathering crowd,
one night clamoring, one night silent,

displays its collection of plumbing
and locks, glass and rust.

We lie underneath unsure
what to claim.

Pickings

The ferocity of those curbside piles,
strewn life. Walking, I stopped to poke through
tangled Christmas lights, splayed paperbacks
heaps of cowboy shirts, violets, blues,
fringes flattened, gooseneck lamp, CDs,
                bicycle pump, jeans

hurled, I thought, by the furious
armful or perhaps – I glanced up – a shot out the
second-story window thrown wide to scream Take him,
take every
                intoxicated by the power of expulsion.
Somewhere in the night those fringes flew
in ecstatic circles, those jeans loved and watched
                and touched and mouthed

        Fury, lonely as the huffing furnace
turned off for the last time. Window empty
apartment bare. Only hunger unremovable
        these gouged entrails picked over by us crows
because there are always crows

at every wake. I carried home shirts, jeans,
        handfuls of him churned through the washer,
collars and cuffs, folded, smoothed, mother-of-pearl buttons,

drove to Goodwill, trafficking in parts, the tough parts
where only tenderness can gnaw through misery

and strangers carry home the bones.

4

Three Boats and a Silence

1

When Otto told me about the Danish resistance smuggling
Jews to Sweden in fishing boat holds slippery with guts

how they wouldn't take anyone who couldn't follow
the dagger-eyed command for silence

no one with a cough, no babies
drawing German lights toward sound

I couldn't get that out of my mind.
Every time I felt a sneeze coming on

I wondered if mortal fear could silence
the body or if I would be the one, wet

and foul with entrails, to send
our group to Theresienstadt.

2

This boat came fast and sudden, summoned, spectral.
The night my mother died the ferryman appeared

sweeping his long oar, his back to me, pulled
by a moon I couldn't dislodge. I heard nothing

only saw. It came to my bed but rests
inside me, damp. No sea so permanent.

I still see it, fog-draped on cold nights
when the house creaks like a wooden

oarlock, the boat always leaving
a long way from waking.

3

People are always disappearing, little
warning and too many vacant rooms.

I don't know why I'm here, not there
or how to salve our brief urgencies.

To let so many people disappear
into a distant dark as if returning takes place

in another land, unfathomable to those
seeking rescue, wave-sloshed and shouting

above the din, safety just beyond the shoals.
I promised a third boat and it, too, has arrived

and disappeared. You'll have to conjure it from
your own Lazarus-act of delivery.

It's easy, like lifting the door of a hold
to shine a light inside.

Morning Walk

> "Genetics, like any language, is built out of basic structural elements – alphabet, vocabulary, syntax, and grammar. The 'alphabet' of genes has only four letters: the four bases of DNA – A, C, G and T."
> — Siddhartha Mukherjee, *The Gene: An Intimate History*

At first light
A breaking open, having learned last night of M's death
The urge to toss aside blankets, slip out

> a slight change in the structure of a receptor that signals excitement to the brain can cause a greater likelihood of impulsiveness in that person

Creaky door, deep breath of pine and mud
An earthy scent this morning I need like I need

> chromosome eleven has a stretch of 155 genes that each encode for a protein receptor that binds with a particular chemical structure to produce the sensation of smell in the brain, such as cinnamon, tar, red rose

Certain predictable houses and trees
Anchored, I don't know what I expected, I keep
Glancing back
Checking, more
Accurately, everything I see seems unreliable

> there is no gene for bewilderment

Those doorways and porches, ragged thistle and
Aloe scrape inside me the way
Time does, living in the body, our
Cells with their own minute

Clocks, exquisitely tuned, that
Cataclysm of time we leave each
Time we leave a room. I left
An open book on the bed where I'd marked pages
To reread
They seem trivial, then urgent
Their message waiting
There is more
Than I imagine
Going on
A whole chorus
And I'm sleepwalking
Through
This daily undoing, lungs, heart, bones, until we leave

> most genes simply increase the likelihood of a certain outcome, mixing with other variables – environment, culture, choices, chance – to produce the variations in personality, temperament, behavior or health that make each person unique

A morning
This morning.

Towhee on the Flagstone

Her stiff hop hop, like a kid in a sack,
cock, cock of her mechanically adjusting head,
laser-eye appraising, beak-pinched weed strands
quivering like whiskers

tell me she is not ready to join
the vanishing beetles, moths, bees,
this rust-streaked, brown-headed cagey
little hopper now under the patio table
strategic as any general's stealth assault.

                    A bullet-fast
shot into the bamboo thicket
carrying her long ancestry wisp by wisp
to the nest as if a lone survivor whose
species hinges on her feint

or is it just what she does? I like
the grander drama, in which I collude
to preserve this vestige of the Mesozoic
this victory of the agile and small.
We'll keep the cat in
take the long view
that's our job these days
two in the bush worth
more and
more.

Intelligence

In the lab, an octopus
        reaches an arm to stuff
unwanted food down a drain only
when the human watches

those slit eyes at water level
                      an opening
to the unfathomable, watching us.

We don't watch is the problem, or don't
imagine cunning can be so squishy.

Synapses, a brain in your arm, why not?
Three hearts carried in a bag on the back. I couldn't

do better than to lug extra hearts forever
reminded of their weight

        and presence, why not
become something crafty and strange, it's not like

we have it all figured out. Never old like us, they die
efficiently after coupling

not over-staying,
they smooth slither melt away.

Trinity Mountains

Up here, a wilderness
of stars count the long hours
of existence indifferently.
None hurries, as far

as we can see. Cataclysm
surrounds them. They're
unconcerned as a slow
revolving door heading
the only way it knows,
around and around.

From our spread blanket
we see the centrifuge they are,
the milky streams they
leave in their fierce,

leisurely passage, always
heading out and returning
as my father, pointing to
Orion, once assured.

And now? Immensity
brings its questions.
Of the stars I'm sure
but what of us beneath?
What are we making of
this one, this singular ride?

I could feel the doubt
and belief I'd balled
together start to shred,

like stardust, I guess
you could say, like our
dust, scattered carelessly,
little thought to what holds
bodies together, what is
necessary and could soon
be lost. It didn't help
to know Copernicus
had strained his neck
like us, leaning back
in a stupor of awe,

Kepler, Herschel, and they
were left with unshakable
faith. I stared hard for a
message that didn't appear
only the unnavigable

future, where stars swirl,
explode, die and all we see
is light. Cold slips of sky
came down to lift my hair.
We groped for each other
while gravity held

us here, hard pebbles
in my back. Sky pulled me
into its dizzying vortex,
flattened me with stars.
We didn't stay, left
the mighty to return
to our hutch where we
warmed and touched.

Circling

> "When we look at living creatures from an outward point of view, one of the first things that strikes us is that they are bundles of habits." – William James, *The Principles of Psychology*

I'm far from being the willful animal James imagines
we could be, changing habits like shirts dropped to the ankles.

Each morning the reiterative dramas.
Sunrise, raspy crows.

Bedroom, kitchen, living room
back to bedroom, a strange nameless cycle
performed daily like the jolt
                of another day tossed

on the midden pile, each bony discard thrown
more quickly than the last
                ritual a daily antidote to speed,

today as unfinished as tomorrow
                as the late

light spreading its canvas for a sky-borne hawk
circling the Chinese elm
                hour after hour.

Through the evening, her splitting, rancorous cry
her future nested, I assume, in top-swaying
branches and hidden
           as motives are. So much effort that engines on
                despite and because.

           No philosophy here but the raw act
whirling in a darkening sky.

Dispatch from the Eighth Decade

I've been subpoenaed, forced to account
for the unaccountable –

a mess on my desk, thinning hair
and all my disbelief. Those young
with their plump, their juice
their abandon, clattering
through their lives, not a thought
of contingency.

Regarding sleep, it's a foreign tongue
indecipherable to those, like me
pacing these rooms, fortunate
to have lasted,
        left to wait and wonder

about the when and how
of that other mystery.
The sky shortens. The night
dozes with its little restless animals
granted a stay.

These Days

These days a love poem
has words like endure
or persist or lucky us
this accumulation.

Resentment, forgiveness
like sand blown across a road
cleared and piled and
cleared again.

Did we use shovels
or was there a wind-scattering
when we weren't looking
or trying?

How curious that effort is needed
also effortlessness, that lapse
that gives way to surprise.

There are as many off-chutes
as days and yet
here we are, having
stayed on the one road
we stumbled onto
watching together what
recedes and appears.

A fine day to drive.
Here are the keys.
Let's keep going.

Hospital Dreams

The old dreams wouldn't do. New dreams blew through
from another windless precipice. Like this: a sunlit
hillside trail curving into shade, deep

with unseen trees. My dead mother
leading me like a physical force, joyful,

from sun-warmth to that dark bend,
welcoming me, suddenly young
like she has become. She wants
me to join her, is that it? Not in years

have we walked together. Time has fled
like the weight of pain

she tosses, too cheerful by far.
How can love approach, arms outstretched
and bring such terror? That desire to
clasp me to her chest.
I have stood
in front of distance and seen
nothing beyond my body's small fire,
shaky, wind-blown.

She hands me my dream like a blanket laid out
for a picnic   fear collapsed into gladness

her joy at my company
which is to say my loss
she can no longer
recognize.

The blanket extends beyond seeing. She lifts
one corner to reveal a staggering
dark, as if ready
to tuck me in.

I wonder how long she waits
at the entrance, those arms
this welcome.

Laws of Motion
    For L.R.

Click at the bottom of the screen to read Larry's paper
on the climate crisis, finished two days
before he died.

Zoom memorial, that Escher-loop of time
able to lift him back on this sun-glittered day
in California, chilly in Boston, and why

shouldn't our faces, mostly grey-haired, expectant,
cross time and space as he does,
      corporal or not we're all
fighting the cold that descends
like a closed eye

      we're all trying to resurrect what flew
through, swiftly, everyone joined
and laughing
      today at the service

celebrating even, having found a way
to enter that room that no longer
      exists, wander around, discover his
bespectacled grin and wild shirt, big hand grasping
      his wife, as if the laws of this world

are some cock-eyed story
no one believes.

We were lulled and then we woke.
We peered into screens as through
the bottom of a hole.

I sent a note to his family after the service.
We all did, missives from people mourning,
confused and continuing, on a planet
still burning.

To Carve

A turkey
        territory
                initials in deadened bench-wood
                              still there
          years since our fingers worked those gashes
          together

the mind in its salvaged parts

a deal, the winter sky into   its cold crystals
falling shards

a bone becomes a deer

                knife scraping clear what's no longer
                            needed

carve a pumpkin, a future
              who can tell me what coheres

a heart that lives beyond its desecration, this afternoon

I'd like to know.

To Whom It May Concern

At the Google conference the speaker breathless
about we'll be able to order a Wendy's hamburger
with AI and it will be exactly as we want. Why
should I be surprised?

Those who can sweep history forward will.
The rest, churned by that wind, hamburger
in hand. Or not. I felt despair, unhelpful
I know, but there it is. Please don't order

a Wendy's burger with AI, please don't tell me
that existential threat will make my life easy
as a thought. I'm bitter, unrepresented
in this plunge toward a future making
someone rich while we
slip
        between fake and real, avatar,
flesh, otherness. It's not possible to rewind
or wrench nostalgia from its corners, even
if I wanted. I do want, I do want better than
what's coming and the front desk
isn't answering.

Afterlife

1

What everyone hurled over
the watery lake-edge

drought returns, stark
and unforgiven.

Coiled bed springs, Chevy cab
mucking up from mud, skeletal

windows washed through
by a receding lake

too changeable for the eternity
needed to forget

who slept in that bed long
drifted away

who turned their back
on the unsalvageable.

2

Science of the left behind means
exact carbon dating of ditch-grass seeds
embedded in fossilized human footprints.
To insist on certainty.
Late Pleistocene. Ice-age lake
in New Mexico.
        In sediment at lake's edge
their imprint mid-stride, exposed
by drought and water drop.

Children, adolescents, their ragged-breath
play. *We are here.* Their afternoon,
Earth's muddy toes being and
vanishing, 61 prints stepping
out of the world they made,
or so it seems.

Of the billions gone we have these 61,
random as the world we're given
and as wondrous.

The marvel of a perfect sole, shape of ourselves
stepping toward what we've become.

3
The thought comes of my grandmother
dying at 102, 11 days before 9/11,
spared the future. What each of us
is not required to bear.
Who will discover us, recover us?
Who will pick through
what we leave on these wet banks

before our exit? Shattered concrete,
mangled steel, plastic-swarmed oceans.
Who will view us with wonder?

Notice

I've been trying to notice beauty
which is everywhere the sky is.

When truth sits like a weight,
indifferent, that's

where I turn, an eye
tipped upward.

Crimson clouds sculling east
on their smooth river

something bright or illuminated
above us

the opposite of resignation
not yet defeated the way a city

can be or a dying river
letting us believe whatever

glimmers up there can shine
down here.

I saw a fat crow this morning
being crow on high wire

where we all live
when you think about it

this high-wire act we convince
ourselves is ordinary,

like a crow feels at home
wire-swaying, sleeping even.

Crow sleep. One eye open,
one-half the brain alert

until the brood shuffles
and the next sentinel lifts

one eyelid in recognition
of precariousness.

There's a constancy
about these birds,

their feathered
huddle against peril,

their sharp cries.
That, too, beauty.

22nd Century Poems

They'll be about planting
not reaping
or weeping

they will have enough tears for every
variety of desperation, dusty
deserted, sea-locked

salt water rising like heat.
As they sow
so shall they

The things we didn't attend
are theirs, endless rows
of our derangement laid at their feet

They carry the pail
daylight fills, never
fast enough

Shocking, the lack of time for recrimination
time needed to carry that pail to water each seedling
under a perilous sky.

The job: to douse
The job: to plant
each morning beginning
again.

The Fight We Have Left

Won't stop at nightfall
won't grind down

like a stone thrashed
by tides, won't lapse,

or be denied. This fight
cannot be taken from us,

we will pass it, one to another
inflamed by kindness

or the desire for kindness
or the insistence

that kindness not be futile
we don't use the word futile, or furious

though we are furiously holding out our hands
with their stone of hope

we won't let go.

Acknowledgments

My thanks and deep appreciation to Bill, my first and best reader, who always makes my poems better. Thanks to Lisa, Zane and Zoe for being who you are and for gracing my life and some of these poems. Special thanks to Diane Frank and Melanie Gendron at Blue Light Press for their patience, skill and enormous support for poets, and much appreciation to Mel Davis for her cover art and artistic insights. Thanks to the following journals in which several of these poems first appeared, some in earlier versions:

Schuylkill Valley Journal: "Between," "Towhee on the Flagstone"

Eastern Iowa Review: "Haiku"

Split Rock Review: "My Grandson Wants to Go to Chernobyl"

Twelve Winters Journal: "Family History"

Persimmon Tree: "Slippage" (under the title "Night by Night")

Midway Journal: "Refrigerator on the Freeway," "Three Boats and a Silence"

"Three Boats and a Silence" was nominated for Sundress Publications Best of the Net Anthology, 2021

Talking River Review: "Hemingway Puts Down His Gun"

Sisyphus: "The Fight We Have Left"

These poems first appeared in the anthology, *Pandemic Puzzle Poems*, Diane Frank and Prartho Sereno, Editors: "Spread," "Shelter"

About the Author

Dorothy Wall is author of *Identity Theory: New and Selected Poems* (Blue Light Press) and *Encounters with the Invisible: Unseen Illness, Controversy, and Chronic Fatigue Syndrome* (Southern Methodist University Press), and coauthor of *Finding Your Writer's Voice: A Guide to Creative Fiction* (St. Martin's Press). Her poetry has been nominated for Best of the Net, and her poems and essays have appeared in magazines and anthologies, including *Prairie Schooner, Witness, Bellevue Literary Review, Sonora Review, Cimarron Review, AMA Journal of Ethics, California Magazine, The Writer, Dos Passos Review, Nimrod, Puerto del Sol, San Francisco Chronicle* and others. She has taught poetry and fiction writing at Napa Valley College, San Francisco State University, and U.C. Berkeley Extension, and works as a writing coach in Oakland. Visit her at www.dorothywall.com.

www.ingramcontent.com/pod-product-compliance
Lightning Source LLC
Chambersburg PA
CBHW031159160426
43193CB00008B/441